The Spirit of Turkey

101 Simple and Delicious Turkish Recipes for the Entire Family

Bryan Rylee

Copyright © by Bryan Rylee.

All rights reserved. No part of this book
May be used or reproduced in any matter
Whatsoever without permission in writing from
The author except in the case of brief quotations
Embodied in critical articles or review.

The information presented in this book represents the views of the publisher as of the date of publication. The publisher reserves the rights to alter update their opinions based on new conditions. This report is for informational purposes only. The author and the publisher do not accept any responsibilities for any liabilities resulting from the use of this information. While every attempt has been made to verify the information provided here, the author and the publisher cannot assume any responsibility for errors, inaccuracies or omissions. Any similarities with people or facts are unintentional.

Table of Contents

Introduction 8
Turkish Cuisine – Common Ingredients...................... 9
   Olive oil.. 9
   Rice... 9
   Eggplants 10
   Lentils... 10
   Ground meat 10
   Bulgur... 11
   Cumin 11
   Fresh Herbs.. 12
   Cinnamon 12
   Kaymak – Clotted Cream 13
   Chickpeas 13
   Pistachios and Walnuts.. 14
   Rosewater 14
   Pomegranates... 14
   Sumac 14
   Tomato 15
Breakfast Recipes 16
   Firinda Omelet – Ricotta and Tomato Omelet 16
   Yumurtali Ispanak – Spinach Sauté with Eggs 18
   Patatesli Yumurta - Potato Scrambled Eggs............. 19
   Turkish Crepes 20
   Cheese Stuffed Bread 21
   Eggs with Tomato Sauce 22
   Baharatli Patates – Spicy Baked Potatoes 23
   Feta Borek 24
   Yarimca – Fried Dough Pockets............................... 26
   Cheesy Mushroom Casserole 28
   Patatesli Kek – Potato Skillet Cakes 30
   Sujuk and Eggs Fry Up 31
   Lutenitsa – Eggplant and Bell Pepper Spread 32
   Cilbir - Poached Eggs and Yogurt Sauce 33
   Turkish Sujuk Panini... 34

   Grape Tomato Bake 35
   Poached Eggs with Cheese Sauce 36
   Breakfast Bread and Egg Casserole 37
   Spicy Roasted Bell Pepper Hummus 38
   Classic Hummus 40
   Easy Pita Bread 42
   Turkish Bell Pepper and Tomato Eggs 43
   Tomato and Sumac Spread on Pita Bread 44
   Baked Halloumi with Caraway Seeds 45
   Turkish Cornbread 46
Salads 47
   Domates Salatasi – Tomato Salad 47
   Tabbouleh Salad – Bulgur and Parsley Salad 49
   Lettuce Salad with Sumac Dressing 50
   Tomato and Walnut Salad 51
   Ispanak Salatasi – Spinach Salad with Olives and
   Corn 52
   Grilled Eggplant Salad 53
   Roasted Bell Pepper Salad 55
   Yogurtlu Patates Salatasi Potato Salad with
   Yogurt Sauce 57
   Mixed Salad with Yogurt and Dill Dressing 58
   Nohut Salatasi - Chickpea and Black Olive Salad 59
   Spinach Salad with Tahini Dressing 60
   Yesil Zeytin Salatasi – Green Olive Salad 61
   Gavurdagi Salatasi 62
   Turkish Fish Salad 63
   Bean and Egg Salad 64
   Artichoke Hearts Salad 65
   Mayonnaise Carrot Salad 66
   Broccoli Salad with Yogurt and Sumac Dressing 67
   Bulgur and Roasted Bell Pepper Salad 68
   Borulce Salatasi – Black-eyed Pea Salad 69
Main Dishes 70
   Bulgur Pilaf 70
   Parsley Falafel 72

- Zucchini Moussaka 74
- Kofka – Turkish Meatballs 75
- Sautéed Leeks with Mint and Thyme 76
- Turkish Stuffed Tomatoes 77
- Spicy Oregano Crusted Halloumi 78
- Pide – Turkish Pizza 79
- Bifteki – Turkish Burgers 81
- Marinated Lamb kebabs 82
- White Wine Chicken 83
- Halloumi and Veggie Kebabs 84
- Zucchini and Feta Fritters 85
- Eggplant Pilaf 87
- Lemon and Yogurt Turkish Chicken 88
- Imam Bayildi – Turkish Stuffed Eggplants 89
- Turkish Fish and Tomato Sauté 90
- Lamb Flatbreads with Mint and Yogurt Sauce 91
- Lamb and Apricot Turkish Meatballs 92
- Roasted Eggplant Puree 93

Soups and Stews 94
- Turkish Red Lentil Soup 94
- Toyga Soup – Chickpea and Yogurt Soup 96
- Umak Corbasi – Umak Soup 97
- Badem Corbasi – Almond Soup 98
- Cold Cucumber and Yogurt Soup 99
- Rustic Chickpea Soup 100
- Turkish Spinach and Lentil Soup 102
- Yahni - Turkish Beef Stew 103
- Turkish Lamb and Rice Soup 105
- Walnut Soup 106
- Baked Lamb and Veggie Stew 107
- Turkish Chicken Red Stew 108
- Lamb and Bean Soup 110
- Chickpea and Potato Stew 111
- Turkish Vegetable and Couscous Stew 112
- Spicy Beef Stew with Egg Noodles 113
- Turkish Spiced Chicken Casserole 114

Turkish Eggplant Stew 116
  Yogurt and Chicken Stew 117
  Rice and Lamb Stew in the Oven 119
Desserts 120
  Revani Cake 120
  Pistachio Baklava 122
  Semolina Halva 124
  Muhallebi – Turkish Rice Pudding 126
  Kunefe – Turkish Katayif 127
  Keskul - Coconut and Pistachio Pudding 129
  Poached Spiced Apricots 130
  Turkish Stuffed Figs 131
  Salep – Turkish Rosewater Rice Pudding 132
  Chocolate and Nuts Turkish Delight 133
  Tropical Turkish Delight 135
  Candied Figs 136
  Almond Crème Caramel 137
  Poached Quinces with Kaimak 139
  Candied Butternut Squash 140
Conclusion 141

Introduction

Cooking is an art that has been explored for centuries all over the globe. That's how cuisines were born and how certain nations got to be defined by the food they cook and eat. The Turkish cuisine, next to French and Italian, is one of the oldest cuisines and it showcases a mix of history and culture. And that is precisely what makes it special. It is part of the Turkish culture more than any other cuisine in this world and getting to know Turkey would not be possible without indulging in the Turkish soups and stews or amazing desserts.

Tangy soups, mint flavored lamb stews, honey desserts and delicious salads, you will find it all in this book that aims to be your starting guide in the Turkish cuisine. All you need to know is here, all the recipes you need to get a proper start in the Turkish way of cooking is between these pages. All 100 recipes are easy to make and can be made with ingredients found in most big supermarkets.

All you need is a bold palate that can stand intense flavors. You need to step out of your comfort zone and try unusual combinations that will prove to you how special and delicious the Turkish cuisine is. Put that apron on and get cooking because you have nothing to lose! In fact, you will gain more knowledge on spices, you will redefine your notion of sweet and fragrant desserts, you will learn that lamb meat is a hidden gem and can be truly delicious if cooked properly, and you will get to learn a bit about the Turkish culture which is amazing and enriching.

Turkish Cuisine – Common Ingredients

The Turkish cuisine has a few staple ingredients and I believe that it is very important to know them before starting to cook Turkish. Once you have a good knowledge of these ingredients, there's nothing stopping you from customizing recipes or even creating your own. After all, even a simple, common roast chicken, for instance, can be enriched with a touch of sumac or cumin. The possibilities are endless if you have this information so keep reading and discover what the Turkish cuisine is all about.

Olive oil

I know olive oil is usually associated with Italy or Spain and their cuisines, but if you look on the map, Turkey is a Mediterranean country too, so it's only fair to have olive oil as well. The benefits of using this oil are numerous, from healthy fatty acids to improved digestion and even cosmetic uses. It's a type of oil that is best used in its most natural form, uncooked if needed, but you can make exceptions and use it in cooking as long as it's not high heat cooking or deep frying. It tends to burn easily so it is not suited for frying.

Rice

Having a stock of rice is a must in a Turkish cuisine because it is such a versatile ingredient. Plus, it is used to make one of the Turkish staples, pilaf, and can be combined with literally any other food, from soups to stews and desserts. It's very easy to store, as well, so make sure you always have it in your pantry.

Eggplants

There are a few veggies that stand out in the Turkish cuisine, but eggplants are by far some of the most common vegetables used in a wide range of recipes, from dips to soups, stews or casseroles. It's a vegetable that cooks easily and tastes great, so don't avoid it when you go shopping.

Lentils

Lentils, especially the red type, are very commonly used in the Turkish cuisine. You will find them in soups or stews and even salads. They are easy to cook, taste great and have plenty of fibers and minerals. Being so filling, they can be served either for lunch or dinner and can be combined with literally any vegetable and still taste great. Lentils are wonderful ingredients in the Turkish cuisine and you will learn to love them for sure.

Ground meat

Usually lamb or beef, ground meat is a staple of the Turkish cuisine and it is used in a wide range of recipes, from stuffed vegetables to the well know pide Turkish pizza. It's up to you which type of meat you use, but lamb is much more Turkish than beef or pork.

Bulgur

Bulgur is made from durum wheat and it has a high nutritional value, being rich in fibers, mainly. The one you usually buy in stores is usually pre-boiled and it comes in two versions: fine and coarse. They are both suited for salads, stews or pilaf. It can easily replace rice in different recipes and it works even in desserts.

Cumin

Cumin is one of the most used spices in the Turkish cuisine. Like all spices, you need a tiny amount to get an intense flavor. It is available in two shapes: seeds and ground and I recommend grinding your own at home because the flavor will be preserved better. Apart from its amazing flavor, cumin also has various medicinal properties, its main one being boosting digestion.

Fresh Herbs

Fresh herbs are an important component of all cuisines around the globe, but even more in the Mediterranean cuisine. The Turkish cuisine is all about bold flavors that are then toned down with fresh herbs. Parsley, dill and cilantro are used in almost every dish and they taste great, but also boost the nutritional content of that dish.

Cinnamon

Oriental cuisines use cinnamon in both sweet and savory dishes. Cinnamon is considered the spice that enhances all the other flavors and it also has numerous health benefits, both medicinal and cosmetic. It's a great addition to your cooking, although if you're not used to it in savory dishes you might find it slightly odd at first. Your palate can be taught to like it in time if you only add a pinch to your savory recipes.

Kaymak – Clotted Cream

Kaymak is a rich and creamy cream that is made either from buffalo or cow's milk. It has around 60% fat so it's very close to certain types of butter. It is a key ingredient in dishes like kataiyf, but it can also be served with other types of desserts, especially those that are soaked in syrup. A great alternative for kaymak is clotted cream.

Chickpeas

Also known as garbanzo beans, chickpeas are one of the main bean in the Turkish cuisine and it is the key ingredient in dishes like falafel or hummus, but it is also used in soups, stews or salads. It is high in protein, carbohydrates and fibers and sometimes it is served as a snack. I recommend buying it already cooked, in cans, because cooking it takes quite some time. Just read labels well and buy those brands that have a low sodium content.

Pistachios and Walnuts

From all the nuts available all around the globe, walnuts and pistachios are the two main nuts used in the Turkish cuisine. They are rich and fatty and have a strong nutty flavor. They are the main ingredients of some well-known Turkish desserts, such as baklava.

Rosewater

What would Turkish desserts be without rosewater?! They would certainly lack a distinctive flavor. It is the main flavor of many Turkish desserts, from cakes to puddings and the famous Turkish delight. It has an intense aroma so only use a small amount to flavor your desserts.

Pomegranates

Pomegranates are in season just a few months per year, mostly fall and winter, but for the rest of the time you can use pomegranate syrup. They are most often used instead of lemons because they are tangy and tart. The syrup makes an excellent addition to salad dressings and the fresh kernels are used as toppings for salads and even soups.

Sumac

Of all the Turkish spices, sumac is probably the most known. It comes from a tree that grows wild in the Mediterranean countries and it is related to poison ivy, but without being toxic. Sumac is sour, fruity and it makes a nice addition to salad dressing because it pairs well with lemon, vinegar or pomegranate. It can also be used to marinate meat, rice, pilaf and stews. It's all up to you how you use it to flavor your foods.

Tomato

Just like in most Mediterranean cuisines, tomatoes are a staple ingredient and are used in anything, from savory tarts, salads, soups, stews, appetizers or morning meals. Even desserts are made with tomatoes, I'm not kidding. They are an amazing fruit that tastes great when in season – summer time. Even green tomatoes are used either for pickling or in stews. Every recipe that involves tomatoes is juicy and absolutely delicious.

Breakfast Recipes

Firinda Omelet – Ricotta and Tomato Omelet

Time: 35 minutes
Serves: 2-4

Ingredients:
5 eggs
½ cup ricotta cheese
1 ripe tomato, sliced
Salt, pepper to taste
1 pinch cumin powder
2 tablespoons chopped parsley
2 tablespoons vegetable oil

Directions:
1. Mix the eggs with salt and pepper to taste then stir in the cumin powder and parsley.
2. Heat the oil in a skillet and stir in the eggs. Turn the heat on low and top the omelet with tomato slices.
3. Cover with a lid and cook for 10 minutes until set.
4. Serve the omelet warm.

Yumurtali Ispanak – Spinach Sauté with Eggs

Time: 25 minutes
Serves: 2-4

Ingredients:
4 cups fresh spinach, chopped
4 tablespoons vegetable oil
¼ teaspoon cumin powder
2 garlic cloves, chopped
1 shallot, chopped
1 cup canned diced tomatoes
2 eggs
Salt, pepper to taste

Directions:
1. Heat the oil in a skillet and stir in the garlic and shallot. Sauté for 2 minutes then add the spinach and cumin.
2. Cook for 2 minutes then stir in the tomatoes.
3. Adjust the taste with salt and pepper and cook for 10-15 minutes on low heat.
4. Crack open the eggs and drop them in the hot sauce.
5. Cover with a lid and cook just 2-4 more minutes until the eggs are set.
6. Serve warm.

Patatesli Yumurta - Potato Scrambled Eggs

This is a classic Turkish dish that can be made with other vegetables, too. Try some zucchinis or bell peppers instead of potatoes and discover the amazing flavors of vegetable scrambled eggs.

Time: 30 minutes
Serves: 2-4

Ingredients:
4 tablespoons vegetable oil
1 pound red potatoes, peeled and diced
4 eggs
¼ cup heavy cream
2 tablespoons chopped parsley
Salt, pepper to taste

Directions:
1. Heat the oil in a skillet and stir in the potatoes.
2. Cook them on low to medium heat until golden brown on all sides, about 10 minutes.
3. Mix the eggs with the heavy cream, parsley, salt and pepper and pour the mixture over the potatoes.
4. Cook until the eggs are cooked then remove from heat and serve warm.

Turkish Crepes

Just like classic crepes, these are versatile and delicate and can be served with fruits, jams or chocolate sauce and ice cream.

Time: 30 minutes
Serves: 2-4

2 cups flour
2 cups milk
2 eggs
1 pinch salt
½ teaspoon baking soda
¼ cup vegetable oil

Directions:
1. Combine all the ingredients in a bowl and mix very well.
2. Heat a frying pan over medium flame and brush it with oil.
3. Pour a few tablespoons of batter in the pan and mix the pan to evenly coat the bottom of the pan with batter.
4. Cook the crepe until golden brown on both sides.
5. Remove onto a plate and repeat with the remaining batter.
6. Serve filled with your favorite fruits or sauces.

Cheese Stuffed Bread

Time: 25 minutes
Serves: 2-4

Ingredients:
2 small breads, cut in half lengthwise
1 cup crumbled feta
1 cup shredded mozzarella
1 pinch cumin powder

Directions:
1. Fill the breads with the cheese and sprinkle with a pinch of cumin.
2. Place the breads on a heated grill pan and cook just until browned.
3. Serve the breads right away.

Eggs with Tomato Sauce

Time: 25 minutes
Serves: 2-4

Ingredients:
4 tablespoons vegetable oil
5 eggs
½ cup tomato sauce
½ cup crumbled feta cheese
1 pinch cumin powder
Salt, pepper to taste

Directions:
1. Beat the eggs with a pinch of salt and pepper.
2. Stir in the cheese, tomato sauce and cumin then add salt and pepper to taste.
3. Heat the oil in a skillet and pour in the eggs.
4. Cook until set, but mix all the time to ensure a creamy texture.
5. Serve the eggs right away.

Baharatli Patates – Spicy Baked Potatoes

Time: 45 minutes
Serves: 4-6

Ingredients:
2 pounds potatoes, peeled and cut in wedges
1 teaspoon paprika
½ teaspoon dried mint
½ teaspoon ground black pepper
1 teaspoon salt
4 tablespoons vegetable oil

Directions:
1. Combine all the ingredients in a bowl and mix gently.
2. Spread the potatoes in a baking tray lined with parchment paper and bake in the preheated oven at 350F for 40 minutes until tender and golden brown.
3. Serve them right away.

Feta Borek

Borek is a versatile dish made with phyllo dough and a filling of your choice, such as feta or spinach.

Time: 55 minutes
Serves: 6-8

Ingredients:
1 package phyllo dough sheets
2 cups crumbled feta cheese
3 eggs
¼ cup chopped dill
1 pinch ground black pepper
½ cup olive oil

Directions:
1. Mix the cheese with the egg, dill and black pepper.
2. Take the phyllo dough sheets and layer them with the feta filling in a deep dish baking pan.
3. Finish with dough and brush with olive oil.
4. Bake in the preheated oven at 350F for 30-40 minutes or until golden brown and crisp on the surface.
5. Remove from the oven and let them cool down before serving.

Yarimca – Fried Dough Pockets

This is a very versatile recipe considering that you can fill these pockets with anything, from cheese to spinach to meat. The dough is tender and flavorful and the final result is a dish that tastes great for breakfast.

Time: 45 minutes
Serves: 4-6

Ingredients:

Dough:
2 ½ cups all-purpose flour
½ cup yogurt
1 egg
1 pinch salt
1 teaspoon baking powder
½ cup cold water

Filling:
2 cups crumbled feta
2 tablespoons chopped dill
1 pinch cumin powder

2 cups vegetable oil for frying

Directions:
1. To make the dough, combine all the ingredients in a bowl and mix well.
2. Transfer onto a well-floured working surface and knead a few times until the dough is elastic.

3. Roll into a large sheet then cut large rounds with a cookie cutter.
4. For the filling, mix the cheese with dill and cumin.
5. Spoon the filling onto each circle of dough and seal the edges together, trapping the filling in.
6. Heat the oil in a pot and drop the pockets in. Fry them until golden brown and serve them warm or chilled.

Cheesy Mushroom Casserole

Time: 45 minutes
Serves: 4-6

Ingredients:
2 pounds mushrooms, sliced
4 garlic cloves, chopped
4 tablespoons vegetable oil
2 green onions, chopped
2 tablespoons chopped parsley
4 eggs
½ teaspoon cumin powder
½ cup crumbled feta cheese
½ cup shredded mozzarella

Directions:
1. Heat the oil in a large skillet and stir in the garlic and green onions. Cook for 2 minutes then add the mushrooms.
2. Sauté for 10 minutes then remove from heat and set aside to cool down.
3. Transfer the mushrooms into a deep dish baking pan.
4. Stir in the eggs, parsley and cumin then top with cheese.
5. Bake in the preheated oven at 350F for 30 minutes.
6. Serve the casserole warm preferably.

Patatesli Kek – Potato Skillet Cakes

Time: 35 minutes
Serves: 4-6

Ingredients:
3 potatoes, peeled and diced
4 tablespoons vegetable oil
1 cup yogurt
1 cup all-purpose flour
2 eggs
¼ cup chopped dill
Salt, pepper to taste
1 tablespoon sesame seeds

Directions:
1. Heat the oil in a skillet and stir in the potatoes.
2. Sauté for 10-15 minutes, stirring often.
3. Mix the yogurt with the eggs, flour, dill, salt and pepper and pour the mixture over the potatoes.
4. Cover with a lid and cook on low heat for 15 minutes.
5. Serve the cake right away.

Sujuk and Eggs Fry Up

Sujuk is a beef sausage that has an intense and specific taste. You can find it at the international or Turkish food isle in most big supermarkets, but if you don't find it, replace it with any other kind of sausage.

Time: 25 minutes
Serves: 4

Ingredients:
2 Sujuk sausages, sliced
4 eggs
2 tablespoons vegetable oil

Directions:
1. Heat the oil in a skillet.
2. Crack open the eggs and drop them in the hot oil.
3. Top with slices of Sujuk and fry the eggs just like you normally do. The sausage will infuse the eggs with an interesting taste.
4. Serve the eggs warm.

Lutenitsa – Eggplant and Bell Pepper Spread

Lutenitsa is a mix between a salad and a spread.It is creamy and incredibly flavorful,given the fact that it has both eggplants and bell peppers.

Time: 30 minutes
Serves: 4

Ingredients:
1 large eggplant, roasted
1 jar roasted bell peppers, drained
1 pinch cumin powder
1 small shallot, finely chopped
Salt, pepper to taste

Directions:
1. Scoop the flesh of the eggplant into a blender and add the bell peppers.
2. Pulse until well blended then stir in the shallot and season with cumin,salt and pepper.
3. Serve the spread with toasted bread.

Cilbir - Poached Eggs and Yogurt Sauce

Time: 20 minutes
Serves: 4

Ingredients:
4 eggs
4 cups water
1 teaspoon white wine vinegar
2 cups yogurt, room temperature
2 garlic cloves, minced
½ teaspoon cumin powder
¼ teaspoon ground coriander
2 tablespoons chopped parsley
Salt, pepper to taste

Directions:
1. Pour the water into a pot and bring it to a boil with the vinegar and a pinch of salt.
2. Crack open the eggs and drop them in the hot water.
3. Cook just 3-4 minutes.
4. In the meantime, mix the yogurt with the garlic, cumin, coriander and parsley in a bowl. Season with salt and pepper to taste.
5. Remove the eggs from the hot water, drain them well and place them in the bowl with the yogurt mixture.
6. Serve right away.

Turkish Sujuk Panini

Sujuk is compulsory, but the other ingredients aren't, so feel free to use kale, bell peppers, Cheddar cheese and whatever spices you want to create these paninis.

Time: 20 minutes
Serves: 2

Ingredients:
2 small breads, cut in half lengthwise
1 sujuk, sliced
½ cup fresh spinach, rinsed
2 slices mozzarella cheese
2 tomato slices

Directions:
1. Fill the breads with sujuk, spinach, mozzarella and tomato slices.
2. Place them in a grill press and cook them for a few minutes until the cheese is melted.
3. Serve the paninis right away.

Grape Tomato Bake

Time: 35 minutes
Serves: 4-6

Ingredients:
6 eggs
½ cup heavy cream
2 tablespoons chopped parsley
½ cup crumbled feta cheese
1 cup grape tomatoes
Salt, pepper to taste
2 tablespoons vegetable oil

Directions:
1. Mix the eggs with the heavy cream, parsley and feta cheese then add salt and pepper to taste.
2. Spread the oil in a skillet and pour in the egg mixture.
3. Top with tomatoes and bake in the preheated oven at 350F for 20-30 minutes until set and fragrant.
4. Serve right away.

Poached Eggs with Cheese Sauce

Time: 15 minutes
Serves: 4

Ingredients:
2 tablespoons butter
2 tablespoons all-purpose flour
2 cups hot milk
1 cup shredded mozzarella cheese
1 pinch nutmeg
4 eggs
Salt, pepper to taste

Directions:
1. Melt the butter in a saucepan and stir in the flour.
2. Cook for 2 minutes, stirring all the time, then gradually pour in the hot milk.
3. Cook until it begins to thicken then add the mozzarella cheese and nutmeg.
4. Season with salt and pepper to taste and remove from heat.
5. Pour a few cups of water in a pot and bring to a boil over medium flame.
6. Crack open the eggs and drop them in the boiling water.
7. Cook them just 3-4 minutes then remove the eggs from the water onto a platter.
8. Top with plenty of sauce and serve right away.

Breakfast Bread and Egg Casserole

Time: 35 minutes
Serves: 4-6

Ingredients:
4 thick slices white bread
6 eggs, beaten
1 tomato, cubed
1 green bell pepper, cored and diced
1 red bell pepper, cored and diced
1 green onion, chopped
2 tablespoons chopped parsley
Salt, pepper to taste
½ teaspoon dried mint

Directions:
1. Place the bread slices at the bottom of a deep dish baking pan and set aside.
2. Mix the eggs with salt, pepper and mint in a bowl. Stir in the rest of the ingredients and pour the mixture over the bread slices.
3. Bake the casserole in the preheated oven at 350F for 30 minutes or until the top is golden brown.
4. Serve the dish warm.

Spicy Roasted Bell Pepper Hummus

Hummus is a well know Oriental dish and it comes in many flavors, this version being one of the most delicious ones. Just give it a try and you will be hooked!

Time: 20 minutes
Serves: 2-4

Ingredients:
1 can chickpeas, drained
1 jar roasted bell peppers, drained
¼ lemon, juiced
¼ cup crumbled feta cheese
¼ cup olive oil
2 garlic cloves
½ teaspoon red pepper flakes
½ teaspoon cumin powder
Salt, pepper to taste

Directions:
1. Combine all the ingredients in a blender and pulse until well blended and smooth.
2. Adjust the taste with salt and pepper.
3. Spoon into a serving bowl and serve right away.

Classic Hummus

You can't say you've tasted Turkish food without the classic hummus made with just chickpeas and tahini paste. It may be simple, but the flavors are delicious!

Time: 20 minutes
Serves: 2-4

Ingredients:
1 can chickpeas, drained
2 tablespoons lemon juice
2 garlic cloves
¼ cup tahini paste
¼ teaspoon cumin powder
Salt, pepper to taste
¼ cup olive oil

Directions:
1. Combine the chickpeas, lemon juice, garlic, tahini and cumin powder in a blender or food processor.
2. Add salt and pepper and process until well blended then gradually stir in the olive oil.
3. Spoon the hummus into a serving bowl and serve it with toasted bread.

Easy Pita Bread

Pita bread is a staple of the Turkish cuisine. In fact, all pastries of this kind are. You can either buy it from a local bakery or make it yourself at home with this easy recipe.

Time: 45 minutes
Serves: 4-6

Ingredients:
3 cups all-purpose flour
2 teaspoons active dry yeast
1 pinch salt
1 cup warm water
¼ cup yogurt
2 tablespoons vegetable oil
¼ cup flour for dusting

Directions:
1. Combine the flour, yeast and salt in a bowl.
2. Stir in the water and yogurt and mix well,then add the oil and knead at least 5 minutes until elastic.
3. Let the dough rest for 10 minutes then split the dough into 4-6 smaller balls.
4. Flour your working surface and roll each piece of dough into a thin round sheet.
5. Heat a non-stick pan over medium flame and place each bread in the skillet.
6. Cover with a lid and cook it 5 minutes on one side. Flip it over and finish cooking a few more minutes.
7. Serve it with hummus or anything else you can think of, replacing your usual bread.
8. Store them wrapped in plastic wrap because they tend to dry easily.

Turkish Bell Pepper and Tomato Eggs

Time: 40 minutes
Serves: 6

Ingredients:
2 tablespoons vegetable oil
1 onion, finely chopped
2 garlic cloves, chopped
1 yellow bell pepper, cored and sliced
1 red bell pepper, cored and sliced
1 green bell pepper, cored and sliced
1 chili, chopped
½ teaspoon cumin powder
1 can diced tomatoes
Salt, pepper to taste
6 eggs

Directions:
1. Heat the oil in a skillet and stir in onion and garlic. Sauté for 2 minutes then add the bell peppers, chili and cumin powder.
2. Cook for 2 more minutes then add the tomatoes.
3. Cook the sauce for 15 minutes, adjust the taste with salt and pepper.
4. Crack open the eggs and drop them in the hot sauce.
5. Cover with a lid and cook 5 more minutes.
6. Serve warm.

Tomato and Sumac Spread on Pita Bread

Time: 20 minutes
Serves: 4

Ingredients:
2 ripe tomatoes, diced
1 shallot, finely chopped
1 green bell pepper, cored and diced
½ cup chopped parsley
1 teaspoon sumac seasoning
1 tablespoon lemon juice
Salt, pepper to taste
4 small pita breads

Directions:
1. Combine all the ingredients in a bowl and mix well.
2. Season with salt and pepper and spoon the spread onto mini pita breads.
3. Serve right away.

Baked Halloumi with Caraway Seeds

Halloumi is an amazing cheese that tastes great baked. You won't be disappointed with such a delicious morning treat like this baked Halloumi cheese infused with the intense aroma of caraway seeds.

Time: 35 minutes
Serves: 2-4

Ingredients:
8 oz. halloumi cheese
¼ cup olive oil
1 teaspoon caraway seeds
2 tablespoons lemon juice
Pita bread for serving

Directions:
1. Place the cheese in a small baking pan and top with caraway seeds, lemon juice and olive oil.
2. Bake the cheese in the preheated oven at 350F for 30 minutes.
3. Serve right away with pita bread.

Turkish Cornbread

Apart from delicious pita bread, Turkish cooks also make an excellent cornbread that can be served with anything from your morning meal to lunch and dinner.

Time: 45 minutes
Serves: 4-6

Ingredients:
1 cup all-purpose flour
1 cup corn flour
2 teaspoon baking powder
1 teaspoon sugar
Salt, pepper to taste
4 eggs
1 ½ cups plain yogurt
2 tablespoons olive oil

Directions:
1. Combine the flours with the baking powder, sugar, salt and pepper in a bowl.
2. Stir in the rest of the ingredients and mix very well then spoon the batter into a baking tray lined with parchment paper.
3. Bake the cornbread in the preheated oven at 350F for 30-40 minutes or until golden brown.
4. Let it cool down in the pan then slice and serve.

Salads

Domates Salatasi – Tomato Salad

It may be a simple recipe, but the sumac makes it truly unique and it is a recipe that is definitely worth a try if you like Oriental flavors.

Time: 20 minutes
Serves: 2-4

Ingredients:
4 ripe tomatoes, sliced
2 cucumbers, sliced
½ cup pitted black olives
4 oz. feta cheese, cubed
4 tablespoons olive oil
2 tablespoons lemon juice

2 tablespoons chopped parsley
Salt, pepper to taste
½ teaspoon sumac

Directions:
1. Combine all the ingredients in a salad bowl.
2. Add salt and pepper to taste and mix gently.
3. Serve the salad as fresh as possible.

Tabbouleh Salad – Bulgur and Parsley Salad

Time: 30 minutes
Serves: 2-4

Ingredients:
½ cup bulgur, rinsed
2 cups vegetable stock or water, hot
1 cup chopped parsley
2 ripe tomatoes, sliced
2 green onions, chopped
1 cucumber, sliced
½ lemon, juiced
Salt, pepper to taste
2 tablespoons olive oil

Directions:
1. Combine the bulgur and hot stock or water in a bowl and mix well then cover with a lid and let it soak up all the liquid.
2. When done, fluff it up with a fork and let it cool down.
3. Stir in the rest of the ingredients then season with salt and pepper to taste and add the lemon juice and olive oil.
4. Mix gently and serve the salad as fresh as possible.

Lettuce Salad with Sumac Dressing

Time: 15 minutes
Serves: 2-4

Ingredients:
1 head lettuce, shredded
1 teaspoon sumac
½ lemon, juiced
2 tablespoons white wine vinegar
¼ cup olive oil
½ teaspoon dried basil
1 teaspoon dried mint
Salt, pepper to taste

Directions:
1. Combine the sumac with the lemon juice, vinegar, olive oil, basil, mint, salt and pepper in a glass jar.
2. Cover with a lid and shake the jar well until the dressing is creamy.
3. Pour the dressing over the shredded lettuce and mix gently.
4. Serve the salad right away.

Tomato and Walnut Salad

Just like in most Mediterranean countries, tomatoes are a big part of the daily menu, especially salads. Tomatoes are combined with many ingredients, but this particular one is truly surprising.

Time: 20 minutes
Serves: 2-4

Ingredients:
4 large tomatoes, cubed
1 teaspoon sumac
½ cup chopped parsley
1 tablespoon pomegranate syrup
4 tablespoons olive oil
1 pinch cayenne pepper
2 tablespoons lemon juice
½ cup chopped walnuts
Salt, pepper to taste

Directions:
1. Combine all the ingredients in a bowl and mix gently.
2. Add salt and pepper to taste and serve the salad as fresh as possible.

Ispanak Salatasi – Spinach Salad with Olives and Corn

Time: 25 minutes
Serves: 2-4

Ingredients:
1 pound fresh baby spinach
½ cup canned corn, drained
½ cup raisins
½ cup pitted black olives
¼ cup chopped walnuts
½ lemon, juiced
1 tablespoon white wine vinegar
1 teaspoon dried mint
Salt, pepper to taste
2 tablespoons olive oil

Directions:
1. Mix the lemon juice, vinegar, mint and olive oil in a glass jar. Add salt and pepper to taste and shake the jar until the dressing is well mixed.
2. Combine all the ingredients of the salad in a bowl and drizzle with the dressing before serving.
3. Serve the salad as fresh as possible.

Grilled Eggplant Salad

You will find many eggplant recipes in the Turkish cuisine. They are all delicious and a good way to discover how great eggplants can actually taste.

Time: 40 minutes
Serves: 2-4

Ingredients:
2 eggplants, sliced
4 tablespoons olive oil
¼ lemon, juiced
2 garlic cloves, minced
1 teaspoon dried mint
2 tablespoons balsamic vinegar
Salt, pepper to taste

Directions:
1. Combine the olive oil with the lemon juice, garlic, mint, salt and pepper and mix well then brush the eggplant slices with this mixture.
2. Heat a grill pan over medium flame and place the eggplant slices on the grill. Cook them on both sides until browned and tender then transfer them into a bowl.
3. Mix gently and serve the salad as fresh as possible.

Roasted Bell Pepper Salad

Time: 40 minutes
Serves: 2-4

Ingredients:
6 red bell peppers, washed and dried
¼ cup olive oil
1 garlic clove, minced
¼ cup balsamic vinegar
¼ cup chopped parsley
Salt, pepper to taste

Directions:
1. Place the bell peppers on a baking tray and roast them under the broiler for 15-20 minutes, flipping them over often to make sure they roast evenly. They are done when the skin is browned, almost burnt.

2. Remove from the oven and carefully peel off the skin.
3. Remove the core and shred the bell peppers in a bowl.
4. Add the rest of the ingredients and mix well.
5. Serve the salad fresh.

Yogurtlu Patates Salatasi Potato Salad with Yogurt Sauce

Time: 40 minutes
Serves: 2-4

Ingredients:
1 ½ pound red potatoes, washed
2 carrots, grated
1 tablespoon mustard
1 ½ cups yogurt
¼ cup chopped parsley
½ lemon, juiced
Salt, pepper to taste

Directions:
1. Place the potatoes in a pot and cover them with water. Cook them until tender, 20-30 minutes.
2. Drain and rinse under cold water then peel off the skin and cut the potatoes into cubes.
3. Transfer them into a salad bowl and stir in the rest of the ingredients.
4. Season with salt and pepper to taste and mix gently then serve the salad fresh.

Mixed Salad with Yogurt and Dill Dressing

Time: 25 minutes
Serves: 2-4

Ingredients:
1 package mixed greens
4 mint leaves, chopped
4 basil leaves, chopped
¼ cup chopped parsley
2/3 cup yogurt
1 teaspoon honey
1 minced garlic clove
Salt, pepper to taste
½ cup chopped walnuts

Directions:
1. Mix the yogurt with the mint, basil, parsley, garlic, honey, salt and pepper to make the dressing.
2. Place the greens on a platter. Top with walnuts and drizzle with the dressing you made earlier.
3. Serve the salad as fresh as possible.

Nohut Salatasi - Chickpea and Black Olive Salad

Time: 20 minutes
Serves: 2-4

Ingredients:
1 can chickpeas, drained
1 red onion, sliced
½ cup black olives
½ cup crumbled feta cheese
1 cup cherry tomatoes, halved
1 teaspoon dried mint
1 teaspoon dried basil
Salt, pepper to taste
2 tablespoons olive oil
2 tablespoons lemon juice

Directions:
1. Combine all the ingredients in a bowl.
2. Add salt and pepper to taste and drizzle with olive oil and lemon juice.
3. Mix gently and serve the salad as fresh as possible.

Spinach Salad with Tahini Dressing

Time: 25 minutes
Serves: 2-4

Ingredients:
1 pound fresh baby spinach
1 red onion, sliced
2 tablespoons tahini paste
¼ cup yogurt
1 garlic clove, minced
2 tablespoons lemon juice
½ teaspoon grated ginger
Salt, pepper to taste
¼ cup chopped walnuts

Directions:
1. Combine the spinach with the red onion and walnuts in a salad bowl.
2. For the dressing, mix the tahini paste with the yogurt, garlic, lemon juice, ginger, salt and pepper in a bowl.
3. Drizzle the dressing over the salad and serve as fresh as possible.

Yesil Zeytin Salatasi – Green Olive Salad

Time: 20 minutes
Serves: 1-2

Ingredients:
1 cup pitted green olives, sliced
½ head lettuce, shredded
1 carrot, finely grated
1 red onion, sliced
1 garlic clove, minced
2 tablespoons olive oil
¼ cup yogurt
1 tablespoon pomegranate syrup
Salt, pepper to taste

Directions:
1. Combine the green olives with the lettuce, carrot and red onion in a salad bowl. Set aside.
2. For the dressing, mix the yogurt with the garlic, olive oil, pomegranate syrup and lemon juice. Add salt and pepper to taste and drizzle the dressing over the salad.
3. Mix gently and serve the salad as fresh as possible.

Gavurdagi Salatasi

Time: 25 minutes
Serves: 1-2

Ingredients:
2 ripe tomatoes, diced
1 shallot, chopped
1 cup chopped parsley
2 tablespoons lemon juice
2 tablespoons olive oil
1 tablespoon pomegranate syrup
1 pinch cayenne pepper
½ teaspoon sumac
Salt, pepper to taste

Directions:
1. Mix all the ingredients in a salad bowl.
2. Add salt and pepper to taste and mix gently.
3. This salad tastes great with kebabs or other meat dishes.

Turkish Fish Salad

Time: 20 minutes
Serves: 2-4

Ingredients:
10 oz. smoked sole fillets, shredded
¼ cup mayonnaise
¼ cup yogurt
1 tablespoon Dijon mustard
2 tablespoons lemon juice
¼ teaspoon chili flakes
1 teaspoon capers, chopped
Salt, pepper to taste

Directions:
1. Combine the mayonnaise with the yogurt, mustard, lemon juice, chili flakes, capers, salt and pepper in a bowl and mix well.
2. Fold in the fish fillets and serve the salad fresh.

Bean and Egg Salad

Time: 20 minutes
Serves: 2-4

Ingredients:
1 can kidney beans, drained
4 hard-boiled eggs, sliced
2 ripe tomatoes, cubed
2 green onions, chopped
½ celery stalk, sliced
1 cucumber, sliced
½ lemon, juiced
2 tablespoons olive oil
½ teaspoon dried mint
½ teaspoon dried basil
Salt, pepper to taste

Directions:
1. Combine the beans with the tomatoes, onions, celery and cucumber in a bowl and mix gently.
2. Stir in the lemon juice, olive oil, mint and basil then season with salt and pepper to taste.
3. Serve the salad as fresh as possible, topped with slices of eggs.

Artichoke Hearts Salad

Time: 20 minutes
Serves: 2-4

Ingredients:
1 jar artichoke heart, drained
1 pound boiled potatoes, cubed
1 red onion, sliced
½ cup kashar cheese, cubed
1 tomato, cubed
4 tablespoons olive oil
1 teaspoon white wine vinegar
1 tablespoon pomegranate syrup
4 tablespoons lemon juice
½ teaspoon dried oregano
Salt, pepper to taste

Directions:
1. Combine the artichoke hearts with potatoes, onion, cheese and tomato in a salad bowl.
2. In a smaller bowl make the dressing by combining the olive oil with the vinegar, syrup, lemon juice, oregano, salt and pepper.
3. Pour the dressing over the salad and mix gently then serve the salad as fresh as possible.

Mayonnaise Carrot Salad

Time: 20 minutes
Serves: 1-2

Ingredients:
2 large carrots, finely grated
1 apple, grated and squeezed out of juice
½ cup mayonnaise
2 tablespoons yogurt
Salt, pepper to taste
1 tablespoon lemon juice

Directions:
1. Combine all the ingredients in a bowl and mix gently.
2. Serve the salad fresh, with kebabs or pita bread.

Broccoli Salad with Yogurt and Sumac Dressing

Time: 25 minutes
Serves: 2-4

Ingredients:
1 large head broccoli, cut into florets
1 cup yogurt
2 tablespoons chopped dill
4 tablespoons chopped parsley
2 tablespoons lemon juice
Salt, pepper to taste
1 pinch cayenne pepper
1 teaspoon sumac

Directions:
1. Cook the broccoli in a steamer or in a large pot of water just for 10-15 minutes until slightly tender.
2. Transfer the broccoli onto a platter and let it cool down.
3. Mix the yogurt with the dill, parsley, lemon juice, cayenne pepper and sumac in a bowl. Add salt and pepper to taste.
4. Pour the dressing over the broccoli and serve the salad as fresh as possible.

Bulgur and Roasted Bell Pepper Salad

Time: 30 minutes
Serves: 2-4

Ingredients:
½ cup bulgur
1 cup hot water
4 roasted bell peppers, chopped
2 ripe tomatoes, diced
1 red onion, finely chopped
½ cup chopped parsley
4 mint leaves, chopped
2 tablespoons pomegranate syrup
4 tablespoons olive oil
2 tablespoons lemon juice
Salt, pepper to taste

Directions:
1. Mix the bulgur with the hot water in a bowl and let it soak up for 10 minutes.
2. When done, fluff it up with a fork and let it cool down.
3. Stir in the rest of the ingredients then add the olive oil, lemon juice, pomegranate syrup, salt and pepper to taste.
4. Mix gently and serve the salad as fresh as possible.

Borulce Salatasi – Black-eyed Pea Salad

Time: 20 minutes
Serves: 2-4

Ingredients:
1 pound fresh shelled black-eyed peas
1 red onion, sliced
4 mint leaves, chopped
½ cup chopped parsley
2 garlic cloves, minced
4 tablespoons olive oil
½ lemon, juiced
½ teaspoon capers, chopped
1 pinch cayenne pepper
4 hard-boiled eggs, sliced

Directions:
1. Mix the black-eyed peas with the onion, mint and parsley in a salad bowl. Set aside.
2. Combine the garlic, olive oil, lemon juice, capers and cayenne pepper in a small bowl.
3. Pour the dressing over the salad and mix gently.
4. Transfer the salad onto a platter and top with egg slices before serving.

Main Dishes

Bulgur Pilaf

Time: 35 minutes
Serves: 2-4

Ingredients:
1 cup bulgur, rinsed
2 tablespoons olive oil
1 shallot, chopped
1 small carrot, diced
1 young zucchini, diced
1 ½ cups chicken stock
2 ripe tomatoes, diced
Salt, pepper to taste
2 tablespoons chopped parsley

Directions:
1. Heat the oil in a heavy saucepan and stir in the shallot and carrot. Sauté for 5 minutes then stir in the zucchini and tomatoes.
2. Sauté for 5-10 minutes then add the bulgur.
3. Pour in the stock, season with salt and pepper and cook the pilaf for 10-15 minutes on medium flame.
4. Remove from heat and add the parsley. Serve warm.

Parsley Falafel

Falafel is a staple dish for the Oriental cuisine and Turkish sure know how to make an excellent falafel, flavored with plenty of parsley and a touch of garlic.

Time: 40 minutes
Serves: 4-6

Ingredients:
2 cans chickpeas, drained
1 shallot, chopped
2 garlic cloves, chopped
¼ cup chopped parsley
1 teaspoon ground coriander
½ teaspoon cumin powder

2 tablespoons all-purpose flour
Salt, pepper to taste
1 pinch chili flakes
½ cup vegetable oil for frying

Directions:
1. Combine the chickpeas, shallot and garlic in a food processor and pulse until well mixed.
2. Stir in the parsley, coriander, cumin and flour then add the chili flakes, salt and pepper and mix well.
3. Form small patties of this mixture and place them all aside on a chopping board.
4. Heat the oil in a skillet or frying pan. Place the falafel patties in the hot oil and cook them on both sides until golden brown.
5. Serve the falafel warm.

Zucchini Moussaka

Moussaka is usually made with potatoes, but this version is much lighter and healthier. Feel free to use potatoes though. It's all up to you.

Time: 1 ¼ hours
Serves: 6-8

Ingredients:
3 zucchinis, sliced
3 onions, chopped
1 ½ pound ground beef
4 tablespoons olive oil
1 can diced tomatoes
¼ cup chopped parsley
2 cups shredded mozzarella
Salt, pepper to taste

Directions:
1. Heat the olive oil in a skillet and stir in the ground beef.
2. Sauté for 5-10 minutes then add the onions and keep cooking for 10 minutes, stirring often.
3. Stir in the tomatoes and parsley, then season with salt and pepper and cook for 20 minutes.
4. Layer the zucchini slices with the meat sauce.
5. Top with cheese and bake the moussaka in the preheated oven at 350F for 30-40 minutes.
6. Serve the moussaka warm.

Kofka – Turkish Meatballs

Time: 1 hour
Serves: 4-6

Ingredients:
1 pound ground beef
1 pound ground lamb
½ cup breadcrumbs
1 teaspoon ground cumin
½ teaspoon smoked paprika
2 garlic cloves, chopped
¼ cup chopped parsley
2 green onions, chopped
1 teaspoon dried mint
Salt, pepper to taste

Directions:
1. Mix all the ingredients in a bowl. Adjust the taste with salt and pepper and mix very well.
2. Wet your hands and form small balls of this mixture. Place them all on a baking tray lined with parchment paper and bake in the preheated oven at 350F for 30 minutes.
3. Serve the meatballs warm or reheat them days after.

Sautéed Leeks with Mint and Thyme

Time: 30 minutes
Serves: 2-4

Ingredients:
5 leeks, sliced
4 tablespoons olive oil
2 carrots, grated
¼ cup white rice
2 cups water
Salt, pepper to taste
¼ teaspoon dried mint
½ teaspoon dried thyme

Directions:
1. Heat the olive oil in a skillet or frying pan and stir in the leeks.
2. Sauté for 10 minutes then add the carrots and rice.
3. Cook for 5 minutes then gradually pour in the water.
4. Add salt and pepper to taste and season with mint and thyme.
5. Cook until all the liquid has been incorporated and serve the leeks fresh and warm.

Turkish Stuffed Tomatoes

Time: 1 ¼ hours
Serves: 6

Ingredients:
6 medium size tomatoes
1 pound ground beef
¼ cup bulgur
½ cup chopped parsley
1 shallot, chopped
½ teaspoon dried mint
½ teaspoon cumin powder
1 cup vegetable stock
¼ cup white wine
Salt, pepper to taste

Directions:
1. Cut off the top of the tomatoes and scoop out the flesh, leaving the skins intact. Chop the flesh and place it in a saucepan.
2. Mix the meat with the bulgur, parsley, shallot, mint, cumin powder, salt and pepper in a bowl.
3. Spoon the filling into each tomato and place them all in the pan over the tomato flesh.
4. Pour in the stock and white wine and cook the tomatoes on medium flame for 30-40 minutes.
5. Serve them warm.

Spicy Oregano Crusted Halloumi

Time: 25 minutes
Serves: 4

Ingredients:
4 slices halloumi cheese
2 eggs
1 cup breadcrumbs
½ teaspoon cumin powder
1 teaspoon dried oregano
¼ teaspoon chili flakes
½ cup vegetable oil for frying

Directions:
1. Mix the eggs in a bowl and set aside.
2. Combine the breadcrumbs with cumin, oregano and chili flakes.
3. Heat the oil in a frying pan then dip each slice of cheese in egg. Roll the cheese through breadcrumbs and drop it in the hot oil.
4. Fry on one side until golden brown, 2-3 minutes, then flip it over and fry a few more minutes.
5. Serve the cheese warm.

Pide – Turkish Pizza

Time: 1 ¼ hours
Serves: 4-6

Ingredients:
Crust:
2 ½ cups all-purpose flour
½ cup corn flour
2 teaspoons active dry yeast
1 teaspoon honey
1 ½ cups warm water
1 pinch salt

Filling:
1 ½ pounds ground lamb
1 shallot, chopped

1 teaspoon smoked paprika
1 teaspoon sweet paprika
2 tablespoons chopped parsley
Salt, pepper to taste
1 cup grated white cheese

Directions:
1. To make the crust, mix all the ingredients in a bowl and knead a few times until the dough is elastic and easy to work with. Cover the bowl with plastic wrap and let the dough rest for 30 minutes.
2. For the filling, heat a skillet over medium flame and stir in the meat. Cook it for 5-10 minutes then add the shallot and sauté for 10 minutes, stirring often.
3. Add the spices, salt and pepper and cook 2 more minutes then remove from heat and let it cool down.
4. To make the pizza, cut the dough into 4-6 smaller pieces.
5. Roll each piece of dough into a thin oval.
6. Spread part of the meat filling over the dough then wrap the edges of the dough to the center, but leave the center exposed.
7. Top with parsley and cheese and bake in the preheated oven at 350F for 20 minutes or until the edges begin to turn golden brown and crisp.
8. Serve the pizza right away.

Bifteki – Turkish Burgers

Time: 45 minutes
Serves: 6-9

Ingredients:
2 pounds ground beef
1 shallot, finely chopped
4 garlic cloves, chopped
1 egg
½ lemon, juiced
1 cup breadcrumbs
Salt, pepper to taste
6-10 burger buns
Your favorite toppings

Directions:
1. Combine all the ingredients in a bowl.
2. Adjust the taste with salt and pepper then wet your hands and form small patties.
3. Heat a grill pan over medium flame and cook the patties on the grill on both sides until browned.
4. Serve the bifteki on burger buns with your favorite toppings.

Marinated Lamb kebabs

Time: 3 hours
Serves: 4-6

Ingredients:
2 pounds lamb meat, cubed
¼ lemon, juiced
¼ cup olive oil
2 garlic cloves, chopped
1 teaspoon cumin powder
2 cups yogurt
Salt, pepper to taste
2 green bell peppers, cored and cubed
2 red bell peppers, cored and cubed
2 cups cherry tomatoes

Directions:
1. Combine the yogurt with the lemon juice, olive oil, garlic and cumin in a bowl. Add salt and pepper then mix in the meat cubes.
2. Let the meat marinate for 2 hours or even overnight.
3. Place the meat and veggies on wooden skewers, layering them.
4. Heat a grill pan over medium flame and place the kebabs on the grill.
5. Cook them on all sides until browned and fragrant and serve them warm once they're done.

White Wine Chicken

Time: 45 minutes
Serves: 2-4

Ingredients:
2 chicken breasts, cut in fillets
4 tablespoons all-purpose flour
1 teaspoon cumin powder
½ teaspoon dried oregano
4 tablespoons vegetable oil
½ cup white wine
Salt, pepper to taste

Directions:
1. Heat the oil in a skillet.
2. Mix the flour with the cumin, oregano, salt and pepper. Roll the meat through flour and drop it into the hot oil.
3. Fry the chicken on both sides until golden brown then pour in the wine.
4. Turn the heat on low and cook for 10-15 minutes until part of the liquid is absorbed.
5. Serve the chicken warm, with your favorite side dish.

Halloumi and Veggie Kebabs

Time: 30 minutes
Serves: 4-6

Ingredients:
10 oz. halloumi cheese, cubed
2 cups cherry tomatoes
2 yellow bell peppers, cored and cubed
1 cup sliced mushrooms
Salt, pepper to taste

Directions:
1. Place the ingredients on wooden skewers, layering them.
2. Sprinkle with salt and pepper.
3. Heat a grill pan over medium flame and place the kebabs on the grill.
4. Cook on all sides until browned and tender, then serve warm.

Zucchini and Feta Fritters

Time: 30 minutes
Serves: 4-6

Ingredients:
Fritters:
3 young zucchinis, grated
1 cup crumbled feta cheese
¼ cup chopped dill
2 green onions, chopped
2 tablespoons chopped parsley
1 cup all-purpose flour
1 pinch chili flakes
½ cup vegetable oil for frying

Yogurt sauce:
2/3 cup yogurt
1 small cucumber, finely grated
Salt, pepper to taste
2 garlic cloves, minced

Directions:
1. Mix the zucchinis with the cheese, dill, onions and parsley.
2. Stir in the flour and chili flakes.
3. Heat the oil in a skillet then drop spoonfuls of batter into the hot oil.
4. Cook on both sides until golden brown and remove them on paper towels.
5. To make the yogurt sauce, combine all the ingredients in a bowl.
6. Serve the fritters dipped in the sauce.

Eggplant Pilaf

Time: 40 minutes
Serves: 4-6

Ingredients:
1 eggplant, peeled and cubed
4 tablespoons olive oil
1 onion, finely chopped
1 ½ cups basmati rice
2 ripe tomatoes, diced
1 teaspoon dried mint
2 cups vegetable stock
1 cup water
Salt, pepper to taste

Directions:
1. Heat the olive oil in a heavy saucepan and stir in the eggplant.
2. Saute for 10 minutes, stirring often, then stir in the onion and rice.
3. Cook for 5 more minutes then add the tomatoes, stock and water.
4. Season with salt, pepper and mint and cook the pilaf for 30 minutes until most of the liquid has been absorbed.
5. Serve the pilaf fresh.

Lemon and Yogurt Turkish Chicken

Time: 2 hours
Serves: 2-4

Ingredients:
2 pounds boneless chicken thighs
1 cup yogurt
Juice and zest from 1 lemon
½ teaspoon dried mint
1 teaspoon dried rosemary
1 pinch dried nutmeg
½ teaspoon cumin powder
1 red pepper, chopped
2 tablespoons olive oil
Salt, pepper to taste

Directions:
1. Mix the yogurt with all the herbs and spices in a bowl.
2. Stir in the olive oil then add salt and pepper to taste.
3. Mix in the meat and let it marinate for at least 1 hour, preferably overnight.
4. Remove the meat from the marinade and place it on a baking tray.
5. Bake the chicken in the preheated oven at 350F for 30-40 minutes.
6. Serve the meat fresh and warm with your favorite side dish.

Imam Bayildi – Turkish Stuffed Eggplants

Time: 1 ¼ hours
Serves: 4

Ingredients:
2 large eggplants, cut in half lengthwise
4 tablespoons olive oil
2 onions, finely chopped
4 garlic cloves, chopped
2 ripe tomatoes, diced
1 teaspoon dried mint
½ cup chopped parsley
2 tablespoons fresh lemon juice
1 teaspoon sugar
½ teaspoon cumin powder
Salt, pepper to taste
1 cup shredded mozzarella cheese

Directions:
1. Scoop out the flesh of each half of eggplant and chop it finely. Set aside.
2. Heat the oil in a skillet and stir in the chopped eggplant and onions.
3. Sauté them for 10 minutes, stirring often, then stir in the rest of the ingredients and season with salt and pepper to taste.
4. Spoon the filling back into each eggplant half and place each half in a baking tray.
5. Top with shredded cheese and bake in the preheated oven at 350F for 30-40 minutes until the cheese is melted and golden brown.
6. Serve the eggplants warm.

Turkish Fish and Tomato Sauté

Time: 35 minutes
Serves: 4

Ingredients:
4 white fish fillets
2 tablespoons olive oil
4 ripe tomatoes, diced
2 red bell peppers, cored and diced
2 garlic cloves, chopped
1 shallot, chopped
1 cup vegetable stock
Salt, pepper to taste
½ lemon, juiced
1 pinch cumin powder

Directions:
1. Heat the oil in a skillet and stir in the shallot and garlic. Sauté for 2-3 minutes then add the bell peppers, tomatoes and stock.
2. Season with salt and pepper and add the cumin powder. Bring this sauce to a boil and cook for 10 minutes.
3. Add in the fish fillets and cook 15 more minutes on low heat.
4. Adjust the taste with lemon juice and serve the sauté warm.

Lamb Flatbreads with Mint and Yogurt Sauce

Time: 45 minutes
Serves: 4

Ingredients:
4 medium size flat breads
1 pound ground lamb
2 tablespoons olive oil
1 shallot, chopped
2 garlic cloves, chopped
1 ripe tomato, diced
¼ teaspoon cayenne pepper
Salt, pepper to taste
2/3 cup yogurt
6 mint leaves, chopped
1 garlic clove, chopped

Directions:
1. Heat the olive oil in a skillet. Stir in the meat and sauté for 5 minutes then add the shallot, garlic, tomato and cayenne.
2. Adjust the taste with salt and pepper and cook until the liquid evaporates.
3. Spread this mixture over the flat breads and cook in the preheated oven at 400F for 10 minutes.
4. For the sauce, mix the yogurt and garlic in a bowl. Add salt and pepper to taste.
5. To serve, drizzle the flat breads with yogurt and serve warm.

Lamb and Apricot Turkish Meatballs

As unusual as it sounds, the apricots make these meatballs a real delight for your senses. Just a bite and you are hooked!

Time: 45 minutes
Serves: 4-6

Ingredients:
2 pounds ground lamb
4 garlic cloves, minced
1 red onion, finely chopped
1 teaspoon ground coriander
1 teaspoon cumin powder
½ teaspoon sumac
1 teaspoon dried mint
4 tablespoons chopped parsley
½ cup dried apricots, chopped
¼ cup breadcrumbs
1 egg
Salt, pepper to taste

Directions:
1. Mix the meat with salt and pepper then stir in the garlic, onion, mint and spices.
2. Mix well and add the parsley, apricots, breadcrumbs and egg.
3. Wet your hands and form small meatballs. Place them on a baking tray lined with parchment paper.
4. Bake the meatballs in the preheated oven at 350F for 30-40 minutes.
5. Serve them right away with your favorite side dish or even freeze them to serve later.

Roasted Eggplant Puree

Time: 1 hour
Serves: 2-4

Ingredients:
2 large eggplants
2 garlic cloves, minced
2 tablespoons tahini paste
¼ cup olive oil
1 shallot, finely chopped
Salt, pepper to taste
Toasted bread to serve

Directions:
1. Cut the eggplants in half lengthwise and sprinkle them with salt and pepper. Spread the garlic over the cut and roast the eggplants in the preheated oven at 400F for 30 minutes.
2. When done, spoon out the soft flesh into a bowl and stir in the tahini paste.
3. Gradually add the olive oil then stir in the shallot and season with salt and pepper.
4. Serve the puree with toasted bread.

Soups and Stews

Turkish Red Lentil Soup

Time: 35 minutes
Serves: 4-6

Ingredients:
2 tablespoons olive oil
1 onion, chopped
1 garlic clove, chopped
1 carrot, diced
1 cup chopped green beans
1 cup dried red lentils, rinsed
1 teaspoon smoked paprika
1 cup diced tomatoes
4 cups vegetable stock or water

½ teaspoon dried mint
Salt, pepper to taste
½ lemon, juiced

Directions:
1. Heat the olive oil in a skillet and stir in the onion and garlic. Sauté for 2 minutes then stir in the carrot, beans and lentils.
2. Cook for 2 more minutes then pour in the stock and add the paprika, mint and tomatoes.
3. Season with salt and pepper to taste and cook the soup on medium flame for 20 minutes.
4. Serve the soup fresh and warm, garnished with lemon juice.

Toyga Soup – Chickpea and Yogurt Soup

Time: 35 minutes
Serves: 4-6

Ingredients:
2 cups canned chickpeas, drained
2 cups vegetable stock
1 cup water
2 cups fresh spinach, shredded
2 garlic cloves, chopped
Salt, pepper to taste
¼ lemon, juiced
1 cup yogurt
1 egg yolk
2 tablespoons all-purpose flour
1 teaspoon dried mint
1 pinch cumin powder

Directions:
1. Heat the stock and water in a pot and stir in the chickpeas, spinach and garlic. Season with salt and pepper and cook for 15 minutes.
2. Mix the yogurt with the egg yolks, flour, mint and cumin in a bowl.
3. Stir this mixture into the soup and cook 5 more minutes until the soup begins to thicken.
4. Serve the soup fresh and warm.

Umak Corbasi – Umak Soup

Time: 30 minutes
Serves: 2-4

Ingredients:
4 cups vegetable stock
1 cup water
1 egg
1 cup milk
1 teaspoon dried mint
2 tablespoons butter
½ cup yogurt
2 garlic cloves, minced
Salt, pepper to taste
¼ cup chopped parsley

Directions:
1. Bring the stock and water to a boil in a soup pot.
2. In a small bowl, mix the egg with enough flour to form a stiff dough. Grate the dough into smaller pieces and throw these pieces in the boiling soup.
3. Add the mint and butter and cook for 10 minutes.
4. Mix the yogurt with the garlic and pour this sauce over the soup.
5. Cook just 5 more minutes then remove from heat and adjust the taste with salt and pepper.
6. Serve the soup warm, topped with chopped parsley.

Badem Corbasi – Almond Soup

Time: 35 minutes
Serves: 2-4

Ingredients:
1 cup almonds, ground
2 tablespoons butter
¼ cup flour
1 ½ cups hot milk
2 cups beef broth
1 pinch nutmeg
Salt, pepper to taste
1 handful pomegranate kernels for serving

Directions:
1. Melt the butter in a soup pot and stir in the almonds and flour.
2. Sauté for 2 minutes then pour in the hot milk and beef, mixing until the soup begins to thicken.
3. Add salt and pepper to taste, but also a pinch of nutmeg.
4. Serve the soup warm, topped with pomegranate kernels.

Cold Cucumber and Yogurt Soup

Time: 20 minutes
Serves: 2-4

Ingredients:
2 cucumbers
2 cups cold yogurt
2 tablespoons lemon juice
Salt, pepper to taste
¼ cup chopped dill

Directions:
1. Mix the cucumber with yogurt, lemon juice, salt and pepper in a blender.
2. Pulse until well blended and smooth then stir in the chopped dill.
3. Serve the soup right away.

Rustic Chickpea Soup

Time: 45 minutes
Serves: 2-4

Ingredients:
1 can chickpeas, drained
1 garlic clove, chopped
1 shallot, chopped
2 tablespoons olive oil
2 ripe tomatoes, diced
1 zucchini, cubed
1 red bell pepper, cored and diced
½ teaspoons dried rosemary
1 teaspoon dried mint
1 pinch cumin powder
Salt, pepper to taste
2 cups vegetable stock
1 cup water
½ lemon, juiced

Directions:
1. Heat the olive oil in a soup pot and stir in the shallot and garlic. Sauté for 2 minutes then add the rest of the ingredients.
2. Pour in the stock and water and adjust the taste with salt and pepper.
3. Cook the soup for 30 minutes then remove from heat and garnish with lemon juice.
4. Serve the soup warm.

Turkish Spinach and Lentil Soup

Time: 40 minutes
Serves: 4-6

Ingredients:
1 cup dried red or green lentils, rinsed
¼ cup olive oil
1 onion, chopped
2 garlic cloves, chopped
¼ teaspoon cayenne pepper
¼ teaspoon cumin powder
1 teaspoon dried mint
2 cups canned diced tomatoes
2 cups chicken stock
2 cups water
¼ cup bulgur
Salt, pepper to taste
¼ cup chopped parsley

Directions:
1. Heat the oil in a soup pot and stir in the onion and garlic. Sauté for 2 minutes then stir in the spices and mint.
2. Add the lentils and tomatoes then pour in the stock and water.
3. Bring to a boil and cook the soup for 15 minutes.
4. Season with salt and pepper and stir in the bulgur.
5. Cook the soup 15 more minutes then remove from heat and stir in the parsley.
6. Serve the soup right away.

Yahni - Turkish Beef Stew

Time: 1 ½ hours
Serves: 4-6

Ingredients:
¼ cup olive oil
2 pounds beef meat, cubed
2 tablespoons flour
½ teaspoon cumin powder
½ teaspoon dried oregano
4 ripe tomatoes, cubed
2 cups pearl onions
2 green bell peppers, cored and diced
2 cups beef stock
2 bay leaves
1 sprig rosemary
Salt, pepper to taste
2 tablespoons chopped coriander

Directions:
1. Mix the flour with the cumin, oregano, salt and pepper to taste.
2. Sprinkle the meat with flour until well coated.
3. Heat the olive oil in a heavy saucepan and stir in the meat. Cook the meat until golden brown on all sides.
4. Add the bell peppers and pearl onions and cook 5 more minutes then stir in the tomatoes and add the bay leaves, rosemary and stock.

5. Turn the heat on low and cook the stew for 1 hour, stirring from time to time. Add more stock if the stew runs out of liquid.
6. When done, remove from heat and sprinkle with chopped coriander.
7. Serve the stew warm.

Turkish Lamb and Rice Soup

Time: 1 ¼ hours
Serves: 4-6

Ingredients:
8 cups water
2 lamb shanks
4 carrots, sliced
2 celery stalks, sliced
1 onion, peeled but left whole
2 garlic cloves, peeled but left whole
1 red bell pepper, cored and coarsely chopped
1 cup long grain rice
Salt, pepper to taste

Directions:
1. Pour the water in a large pot and add the meat. Season with a pinch of salt and cook for 40 minutes on low heat.
2. Stir in the carrots, celery, onion, garlic and bell pepper and cook 20 more minutes.
3. Stir in the rice and keep cooking 15 more minutes.
4. Remove and discard the onion and garlic and serve the soup warm and fresh.

Walnut Soup

This clearly is not a soup that many people know about, but go out of your comfort zone and give it a try. You will be surprised to discover a savory, rich soup that has a unique taste and flavor.

Time: 35 minutes
Serves: 4-6

Ingredients:
1 cup chopped walnuts
2 tablespoons olive oil
2 onions, chopped
2 garlic cloves, chopped
2 oranges, zested and juiced
1 pinch cumin powder
4 cups vegetable stock
1 cup yogurt
Salt, pepper to taste
¼ cup chopped parsley

Directions:
1. Heat the olive oil in a soup pot and stir in the onions and garlic. Sauté for 5 minutes then stir in the walnuts, orange juice, orange zest and cumin powder.
2. Pour in the stock and cook for 20 minutes.
3. Puree the soup with an immersion blender then season with salt and pepper to taste.
4. Pour the soup into serving bowls and top with chopped parsley.
5. Serve it right away.

Baked Lamb and Veggie Stew

Baking is the real trick for a delicious stew. Cooking it in the oven at low heat allows the flavors to develop and the final result is a real delight.

Time: 4 hours
Serves: 4-6

Ingredients:
2 pounds boneless leg of lamb, cubed
2 red onions, sliced
4 garlic cloves, chopped
6 ripe tomatoes, sliced
1 pound mushrooms, sliced
2 large potatoes, peeled and cubed
½ pound green beans, chopped
1 zucchini, sliced
Salt, pepper to taste
2 cups vegetable stock
2 bay leaves
1 teaspoon cumin powder
¼ teaspoon cinnamon powder
Salt, pepper to taste

Directions:
1. Combine all the ingredients in a heavy pot that can go in the oven.
2. Season with salt and pepper to taste and cook the stew in the preheated oven at 300F for 3-4 hours.
3. It is done when the meat shreds easily.
4. Serve the stew warm with your favorite side dish, although the vegetables may be enough.

Turkish Chicken Red Stew

Time: 1 hour
Serves: 4-6

Ingredients:
1 whole chicken, cut in smaller pieces
1 red onion, chopped
4 garlic cloves, chopped
4 tablespoons olive oil
4 roasted red bell peppers, chopped
2 carrots, peeled and sliced
4 ripe tomatoes, diced
Salt, pepper to taste
1 teaspoon smoked paprika
½ teaspoon cumin powder
Salt, pepper to taste
1 ½ cups chicken stock
1 bay leaf

Directions:
1. Heat the oil in a heavy pot and add the onion and garlic.
2. Sauté for 5 minutes then stir in the bell peppers, carrots and tomatoes. Cook 5 more minutes then add the paprika and cumin.
3. Pour in the stock then place the chicken in the pot.
4. Add the bay leaf, season with salt and pepper and cover the pot with a lid.
5. Cook the stew for 40-50 minutes on low heat.
6. Serve the stew warm with your favorite side dish.

Lamb and Bean Soup

Time: 2 hours
Serves: 4-6

Ingredients:
1 ½ pounds lamb meat, cubed
2 tablespoons olive oil
2 cups dried white beans, rinsed
6 cups vegetable stock
2 onions, chopped
1 can diced tomatoes
Salt, pepper to taste
½ teaspoon chili flakes
½ teaspoon cumin powder
2 bay leaves
¼ cup chopped cilantro
2 tablespoons chopped parsley

Directions:
1. Heat the oil in a heavy saucepan and stir in the meat. Cook for 5-10 minutes until golden brown then add the onions and sauté for 5 more minutes until translucent.
2. Stir in the beans, tomatoes and stock then season with salt and pepper to taste and add the chili flakes, cumin and bay leaves.
3. Cook the stew on low heat for 2 hours, adding more liquid if it runs out.
4. When done, stir in the cilantro and parsley and serve right away.

Chickpea and Potato Stew

Time: 40 minutes
Serves: 4-6

Ingredients:
1 can chickpeas, drained
4 potatoes, peeled and diced
2 ripe tomatoes, diced
2 red bell peppers, cored and diced
1 onion, chopped
2 garlic cloves, chopped
4 tablespoons olive oil
1 cup vegetable stock
1 cup water
1 bay leaf
Salt, pepper to taste
1 pinch cayenne pepper

Directions:
1. Heat the oil in a heavy pot and stir in the onion and garlic. Sauté until translucent, about 3 minutes, then stir in the potatoes, tomatoes, bell peppers and chickpeas.
2. Sauté for 10 minutes then add the stock, water, bay leaf and cayenne pepper.
3. Season with salt and pepper and cook the stew on low to medium flame for 30 minutes or until the vegetables are tender and the sauce is thick.
4. Serve the stew warm.

Turkish Vegetable and Couscous Stew

Time: 40 minutes
Serves: 6-8

Ingredients:
4 tablespoons olive oil
1 onion, sliced
2 garlic cloves, chopped
1 zucchini, sliced
1 eggplant, peeled and cubed
1 sweet potato, peeled and cubed
4 artichoke hearts, chopped
1 can diced tomatoes
1 can chickpeas, drained
2 bay leaves
½ teaspoon sumac
Salt, pepper to taste
3 cups vegetable stock
1 cup couscous, rinsed
¼ cup chopped parsley

Directions:
1. Heat the oil in a heavy saucepan and stir in the onion and garlic. Sauté for 2-3 minutes then stir in the rest of the vegetables.
2. Sauté for 10 minutes, stirring often, then add the stock, sumac and bay leaves and season with salt and pepper to taste.
3. Cook the veggies for 15 minutes.
4. Stir in the couscous and cook 10 more minutes.
5. Remove from heat and serve the stew warm and fresh, topped with chopped parsley.

Spicy Beef Stew with Egg Noodles

Time: 2 hours
Serves: 4-6

Ingredients:
4 tablespoons butter
1 ½ pound beef meat, cubed
1 pound mushrooms, sliced
2 cans diced tomatoes
1 ½ cups beef stock
¼ teaspoon cinnamon powder
½ teaspoon cumin powder
½ teaspoon sumac
½ teaspoon cayenne pepper
Salt, pepper to taste
10 oz. egg noodles

Directions:
1. Heat the butter in a heavy saucepan and stir in the meat. Sauté for 5-10 minutes then stir in the mushrooms, tomatoes and stock.
2. Add the spices, but also salt and pepper to taste and cook the stew on low heat for 1 ½ hours.
3. When the stew is ready, cook the noodles in a large pot of water just until al dente.
4. Place the noodles on a platter and top with beef stew.
5. Serve right away.

Turkish Spiced Chicken Casserole

Time: 1 hour
Serves: 4-6

Ingredients:
1 whole chicken, cut in smaller pieces
1 onion, chopped
4 garlic cloves, chopped
4 tablespoons olive oil
1 zucchini, sliced
2 potatoes, peeled and cubed
2 sweet potatoes, peeled and cubed
1 can diced tomatoes
1 eggplant, peeled and cubed
2 cups canned black beans, drained
Salt, pepper to taste
2 cups chicken stock
½ teaspoon cumin powder
½ teaspoon cayenne pepper
1 teaspoon sumac
4 bay leaves

Directions:
1. Heat the oil in a skillet and stir in the onion and garlic.
2. Sauté for 2-3 minutes then add the rest of the vegetables and cook for 10 minutes.
3. Transfer the veggies in a deep dish baking pan and pour in the stock.
4. Add the spices and bay leaves and season with salt and pepper.

5. Place the chicken over the veggies and bake in the preheated oven at 350F for 1 ½ hours.
6. Serve the chicken warm.

Turkish Eggplant Stew

Time: 55 minutes
Serves: 4-6

Ingredients:
2 large eggplants, peeled and cubed
1 onion, chopped
2 garlic cloves, chopped
4 tablespoons olive oil
1 zucchini, sliced
4 ripe tomatoes, peeled and diced
¼ cup tomato puree
½ teaspoon sumac
1 cup vegetable stock
Salt, pepper to taste
2 tablespoons chopped cilantro

Directions:
1. Heat the oil in a skillet and stir in the onion and garlic. Sauté for 2-3 minutes then add the eggplants and zucchini.
2. Sauté for 10 minutes then stir in the tomatoes and tomato puree.
3. Stir in the sumac then add the stock, salt and pepper.
4. Cook the stew for 30 minutes on medium flame.
5. When done, stir in the cilantro and remove from heat.
6. Serve the stew warm.

Yogurt and Chicken Stew

Time: 1 hour
Serves: 4-6

Ingredients:
1 ½ pounds chicken breasts, cubed
1 onion, chopped
2 garlic cloves, chopped
4 tablespoons olive oil
2 carrots, peeled and sliced
2 potatoes, peeled and cubed
1 cup tomato puree
2 bay leaves
1 teaspoon dried oregano
¼ teaspoons chili flakes
1 cup yogurt
1 teaspoon cumin powder
2 tablespoons lemon juice
Salt, pepper to taste
Cooked rice to serve

Directions:
1. Heat the oil in a skillet and stir in the meat.
2. Cook until it begins to look golden brown then stir in the garlic and onion.
3. Sauté for 2-3 minutes then stir in the carrots, potatoes, tomato puree, bay leaves, oregano and chili flakes.
4. Add salt and pepper to taste and cook the stew for 30 minutes on low heat.

5. Mix the yogurt with the cumin powder and lemon juice.
6. Pour this mixture over the stew and mix gently. Cook for 5-10 more minutes.
7. Serve the stew warm with cooked rice.

Rice and Lamb Stew in the Oven

Time: 1 ½ hours
Serves: 4-6

Ingredients:
1 ½ pounds lamb meat, cubed
1 onion, sliced
1 zucchini, sliced
1 eggplant, peeled and sliced
2 cups green peas
½ pound green beans, trimmed and chopped
1 cup white rice
4 cups vegetable stock
2 bay leaves
Salt, pepper to taste

Directions:
1. Combine the veggies with the rice and stock in a deep dish baking pan.
2. Season with salt and pepper and add the bay leaves then place the meat over the rice.
3. Cover the pan with aluminum foil and cook in the preheated oven at 350F for 1 hour.
4. Remove the foil and cook for 15 more minutes until it begins to look golden brown.
5. Serve the stew warm.

Desserts

Revani Cake

You won't get any other dessert that is more Turkish than this one. It's sweet, fragrant and juicy, absolutely delicious served chilled.

Time: 1 hour
Serves: 8-10

Ingredients:
6 eggs
1 ¼ cups semolina
1 cup all-purpose flour
1 pinch salt
1 cup sugar
3 cups sugar for syrup
3 cups water
½ lemon, juiced
1 teaspoon rose water
1 teaspoon vanilla extract

Directions:
1. Separate the egg yolks from the egg whites.
2. Whip the egg whites with a pinch of salt until fluffy then set aside.
3. Combine the egg yolks with 1 cup of sugar and mix until they turn creamy and pale in color. Add the vanilla extract then stir in the flour and semolina.
4. Fold in the whipped egg whites then spoon the batter into a baking tray greased with oil or butter.
5. Bake the cake in the preheated oven at 350F for 40 minutes.
6. While the cake is baking, make the syrup by mixing 3 cups of water with 3 cups of sugar.
7. Place over medium flame and add the lemon juice. Cook the syrup for 10 minutes then remove from heat and let it cool down. Add the rose water and mix well.
8. When the cake is done, remove from the oven and let it cool down 10 minutes.
9. Pour the chilled syrup over the cake and let it soak overnight.
10. Slice and serve the cake right away.

Pistachio Baklava

Time: 1 ¼ hours
Serves: 8-10

Ingredients:
1 package phyllo dough sheets
½ cup melted butter
10 oz. ground pistachio
1 cup ground almonds
1 pinch salt

Syrup:
1 cup sugar
½ cup honey
2 cups water
½ lemon, juiced
1 tablespoon lemon zest

Directions:
1. Divide the phyllo sheets in half.
2. Take half of the dough sheets and place them in a baking tray, brushing each of them with melted butter.
3. Mix the pistachio with the almonds and a pinch of salt. Spread the mixture over the phyllo sheets and top with the remaining dough, brushed with butter.
4. Cut the baklava in small squares and bake in the preheated oven at 350F for 40 minutes or until crisp and golden brown.
5. To make the syrup, combine the honey, sugar, water, lemon juice and lemon zest in a saucepan

and bring to a boil. Cook the syrup for 10 minutes then let it cool down.
6. When the baklava is baked, pour the chilled syrup evenly and let it cool down and soak up all the liquid.
7. Serve the baklava chilled.

Semolina Halva

Time: 35 minutes
Serves: 4-6

Ingredients:
1 cup semolina
¼ cup butter
2 tablespoons pine nuts
¼ cup chopped apricots
¼ cup raisins
1 cup sugar
2 cups water
½ teaspoon rose water

Directions:
1. Melt the butter in a saucepan and stir in the semolina.
2. Sauté for 2 minutes, stirring often, then add the pine nuts, apricots, raisins and sugar.
3. Pour in the water and mix well, cooking the mixture for 10-15 minutes until thick and creamy.
4. Remove from heat, stir in the rose water and pour the mixture into serving bowls.
5. Let it cool down completely then serve.

Muhallebi – Turkish Rice Pudding

Time: 35 minutes
Serves: 4-6

Ingredients:
3 cups milk
1/3 cup rice flour
½ cup sugar
1 teaspoon vanilla extract
2 tablespoons chopped candied orange peel
2 tablespoons raisins
½ cup pistachio,chopped

Directions:
1. Mix the milk with the rice flour over medium flame and cook it until it begins to thicken, stirring all the time.
2. Add sugar and vanilla extract and pour the pudding into individual serving bowls.
3. Top with orange peel, raisins and pistachio and serve when chilled.

Kunefe – Turkish Katayif

Time: 45 minutes
Serves: 4-6

Ingredients:
2 cups sugar
2 cups water
1 teaspoon vanilla extract
10 oz. katayif
¼ cup melted butter
3 cups sweet cheese

Directions:
1. Mix the sugar with the water and cook the syrup over medium flame for 5-10 minutes. Remove from heat and let it cool down.

2. Layer the katayif with the cheese in a deep dish baking pan.
3. Drizzle with butter and bake in the preheated oven at 350F for 30 minutes or until the top begins to look golden brown.
4. When done, pour in the sugar syrup and serve the kunefe when chilled.

Keskul - Coconut and Pistachio Pudding

Time: 30 minutes
Serves: 4-6

Ingredients:
4 cups milk
½ cup shredded coconut
2/3 cup sugar
1 egg yolk
¼ cup cornstarch
1 pinch salt
½ cup ground pistachio

Directions:
1. Heat the milk and shredded coconut in a saucepan.
2. In a bowl, combine the sugar with the egg yolk until creamy then add the cornstarch and a pinch of salt.
3. Pour the hot milk over the egg mixture and mix well then transfer the mixture back into the saucepan and cook until it begins to thicken.
4. Pour the pudding in serving bowls.
5. Top with ground pistachio and serve when chilled.

Poached Spiced Apricots

Time: 30 minutes
Serves: 2-4

Ingredients:
1 pound fresh apricots
½ cup dried apricots
¼ cup honey
1 cinnamon stick
1 star anise
4 cups water

Directions:
1. Combine the water with the honey, cinnamon stick and star anise in a saucepan and bring to a boil.
2. Add the apricots and cook them for 15-20 minutes.
3. Remove from heat and let it cool down then pour into serving bowls and serve with ice cubes.

Turkish Stuffed Figs

Time: 15 minutes
Serves: 6

Ingredients:
12 jumbo size dried figs
12 pieces walnuts
¼ cup honey
4 mint leaves, chopped

Directions:
1. Carefully cut open the figs and stuff them with pieces of walnuts.
2. Place them on a platter and drizzle them with honey. Top with a few bits of chopped mint and serve right away.

Salep – Turkish Rosewater Rice Pudding

Time: 30 minutes
Serves: 2-4

Ingredients:
4 tablespoons glutinous rice flour
4 cups milk
¼ cup sugar
2 tablespoons honey
1 pinch cinnamon
1 teaspoon rosewater
½ cup chopped pistachio

Directions:
1. Mix the flour with the milk, sugar and honey in a heavy saucepan and cook until it begins to thicken. Stir all the time to make sure it doesn't burn and maintain a low heat while cooking.
2. Remove from heat and stir in the cinnamon and rosewater.
3. Spoon the pudding into individual serving bowls and top with pistachio.
4. Serve only when chilled.

Chocolate and Nuts Turkish Delight

Turkish delight is a well-known dessert worldwide and although it's easily found in most big stores, you can make your own at home. It's not that hard and it tastes better than any store bought one.

Time: 1 hour
Serves: 8-10

Ingredients:
2 ½ cups water
¼ cup powdered gelatin
2 cups sugar
¾ cup cornstarch
1 cup powdered sugar
2 tablespoons lemon juice
1 teaspoon vanilla extract
1 teaspoon rosewater
3 oz. dark chocolate, melted
1 pinch salt
1 cup mixed nuts, chopped

Directions:
1. Mix the gelatin with the water and let it bloom for 10 minutes.
2. Place the pot on medium heat and stir in the sugar. Cook this syrup until it begins to thicken.
3. Remove from heat and stir in the cornstarch, powdered sugar, vanilla, rosewater and chocolate.
4. Place back on heat and cook on very low heat for 1 more minutes, being careful not to let it boil again.

5. Remove from heat and stir in the nuts.
6. Pour the mixture into a square pan lined with plastic wrap and refrigerate 2 hours at least.
7. Cut into small squares and serve.

Tropical Turkish Delight

Time: 1 hour
Serves: 8-10

Ingredients:
1 ½ cups water
3 cups sugar
¼ cup light corn syrup
½ cup orange juice
2 tablespoons orange zest
¼ cup dried mango, chopped
¼ cup candied pineapple, chopped
¾ cup cornstarch
3 tablespoons gelatin bloomed in ½ cup cold water
1 teaspoon vanilla extract
½ cup shredded coconut for coating

Directions:
1. Mix the water with the sugar, corn syrup and orange zest in a saucepan and bring to a boil. Cook the syrup for 5-10 minutes then remove from heat and add the cornstarch and gelatin.
2. Mix well until the mixture is thick then stir in the mango, orange zest, pineapple and vanilla extract.
3. Pour this mixture into a square baking pan lined with plastic wrap.
4. Refrigerate at least 2 hours before slicing into smaller squares.
5. Roll each square through shredded coconut and serve.

Candied Figs

Time: 30 minutes
Serves: 4-6

Ingredients:
12 large dried figs
1 cup sugar
1 cup water
½ cup fresh orange juice
2 tablespoons honey
½ cup chopped walnuts

Directions:
1. Mix the water with the sugar and honey and cook this syrup for 5-10 minutes.
2. Stir in the figs and cook them just 5 minutes.
3. Remove from heat and spoon into a large serving bowl.
4. Let the figs cool down then top with chopped walnuts and serve.

Almond Crème Caramel

Yes, Turkish love crème caramel. Their twist is adding a touch of almond liqueur into the caramel, thus creating a delicious crème caramel.

Time: 1 hour
Serves: 4

Ingredients:
3 cups milk
4 eggs
4 egg yolks
4 tablespoons sugar
1 cup brown sugar
1 teaspoon almond liqueur or extract

Directions:
1. Melt the brown sugar in a saucepan. When the sugar is melted, stir in the almond liqueur, being careful because it tends to splash.
2. Pour the caramel equally between 4 individual ramekins and move the ramekins to evenly coat their bottom. Set aside.
3. Combine the milk with the eggs, egg yolks and sugar in a bowl.
4. Pour this mixture over the caramel and bake the crème caramel in the preheated oven at 300F for 40 minutes until set.
5. Remove from the oven and let it cool down completely before serving.

Poached Quinces with Kaimak

Time: 30 minutes
Serves: 4

Ingredients:
2 large quinces, peeled, halved and cored
1 cup sugar
3 cups water
2 tablespoons honey
1 cinnamon stick
¼ lemon, juiced
1 lemon peel
1 cup Turkish kaymak

Directions:
1. Mix the sugar with the water, honey, lemon juice, cinnamon stick and lemon peel in a saucepan and bring to a boil.
2. Add in the quinces and cook on medium heat for 20-30 minutes until tender.
3. When done, remove from heat and place the quinces in serving bowls.
4. Keep cooking the syrup left in the pan for 10 more minutes then drizzle it over the quinces.
5. Top with kaymak and serve right away.

Candied Butternut Squash

Time: 30 minutes
Serves: 4-6

Ingredients:
2 cups sugar
2 cups water
2 tablespoons honey
4 cups butternut squash cubes
½ teaspoon vanilla extract
½ cup chopped walnuts

Directions:
1. Combine the sugar with the water and honey in a saucepan and bring to a boil. Cook the syrup until it begins to thicken then add the squash.
2. Keep cooking for at least 10 minutes then remove from heat, add the vanilla and let it cool down.
3. Serve the squash chilled, topped with walnuts.

Conclusion

Each cuisine on the globe has its own characteristics;some are more distinctive, some are more common, but the Turkish cuisine is definitely one of those that can pride itself in being truly unique. The Turkish cuisine is a balanced mix between the Mediterranean cuisines and the Oriental ones. After all, the country itself sits proudly just where two continents collide: Europe and Asia. But what's born from this collision is a culture that impresses, a culture that stood the test of time and still does, a country which attracts each year millions and millions of visitors eager to get a glimpse of the famous Turkish cuisine and learn more about the culture itself.

But you don't have to visit Turkey to know the culture or to taste the food. With this book, you can make all these staple foods in the comfort of your own kitchen. That's how simple it is! SO put that apron on and be ready for amazing flavors and delicious dishes because that is what you will get with this book!